W9-BNA-876

The refrigerator chills your food. The game station powers your video games.
A lightbulb shines on your homework. All of these devices use electricity. To make electricity, we mostly burn coal, oil, or trees. But these fuels are running out. Plus, they **pollute** the air and hurt our planet. The good news is that you can help! There are many ways you can save electricity.

10 Things You Can Do To

Save Electricity

by Jenny Mason

Content Consultant
Nanci R. Vargus, Ed.D.
Professor Emeritus, University of Indianapolis

Reading Consultant
Jeanne M. Clidas, Ph.D.
Reading Specialist

Children's Press®
An Imprint of Scholastic Inc.

Table of Contents

1 Unplug Unused

Many devices waste electricity even when they are off. Computers and televisions are examples of these "energy vampires." Pull the plug on those

Where are the energy vampires in your house?

Devices

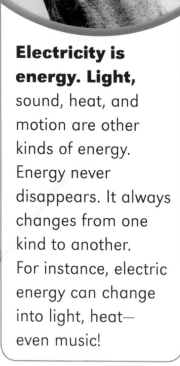

monsters when you are not using them. You can also plug them into power strips that turn off on their own.

Electricity is energy. Light, sound, heat, and motion are other kinds of energy. Energy never disappears. It always changes from one kind to another. For instance, electric energy can change into light, heat— even music!

A power strip can stop the flow of electricity to devices that are turned off.

2 Replace Old

The **incandescent** lightbulb was invented more than 100 years ago. Inside the bulb, electricity heats a tiny metal thread. That creates a bright glow.

Use a desk lamp instead of an overhead lamp. That will save electricity, too.

Lightbulbs

Today, newer types of bulbs use gas or crystals instead. They are brighter and use less electricity. Ask your parents to replace any old bulbs with energy-saving varieties. *CFL* stands for "compact fluorescent lamp." CFL bulbs are more efficient. They use a lot less electricity than incandescent bulbs.

The LED is a type of bulb. *LED* stands for "light-emitting diode." LEDs are eight times as efficient as incandescent bulbs. That is why you find them almost everywhere. They are used in TV screens, traffic lights, and holiday lights!

Burning fuel to make electricity releases greenhouse gases into the air. They trap heat from the sun. If too much heat gets trapped, Earth's temperature begins to rise. Ice sheets melt. Ocean levels rise. The effects of this climate change are felt around the globe. Clean energy does not release greenhouse gases.

Energy

Clean energy includes wind and solar.

Solar energy is the light and heat that come from the sun. A lot of solar energy reaches Earth's surface in just one minute. It is enough to power the whole world for a year. Some of it can be collected with solar panels.

When sea ice melts, polar bears lose their homes and hunting grounds.

Heat Up and Cool

The heater and air conditioner use a lot of electricity to heat or cool your house. The wind and sun use none. When it is hot outside, open the windows to let in a cool breeze. On cold days, keep the windows closed. But open the curtains or blinds. Sunlight will warm the room.

Planting trees around your house can save electricity, too. Trees shade the house in summer and block cold winter winds.

Down Naturally

To stay warm naturally,
get under the blankets
when watching TV.

5 Clean Your

Dirty devices work harder. So they use more power. If you keep your electronics clean, you will save electricity. Wipe dust off computers and TVs.

Dusty electronics are more than just gross to look at. They also waste a lot of electricity.

Electronics

Clean glass covers on ceiling lights to let more light shine out. Remember to clean the lint trap on the dryer, too.

Keeping your devices clean will also make them last longer. Then they won't pile up at the dump. In the U.S., 130,000 computers are thrown away every day. Around the world, trashed electronics make up more than 100 billion pounds (45 million metric tons) of garbage.

Water treatment plants bring clean water to your house. They need a lot of electricity to do that. When you use less water, the treatment plants use less electricity. Shut off the faucet when you brush your teeth. See who can take the fastest shower in your family.

Save Electricity

Electricity that comes from rivers, waterfalls, and dams (like the one pictured) is called hydropower. Hydropower makes 85 percent of all clean energy around the world.

7 Reuse or Repurpose

It takes a lot of electricity to make new clothes or toys. Instead of buying new things, **recycle** what you already have. Use both

Recycling does more than help save electricity. It's fun, too!

Old Things

sides of the paper when you draw. Use a milk jug to store your art supplies. What other crafty ideas can you think of?

Recycling one aluminum can saves enough electricity to power a TV for three hours. And it takes 95 percent less energy to make a can out of recycled aluminum than to make a brand-new can.

A pair of rain boots can become a planter. Old newspapers can turn into pencil cups!

Batteries power a lot of the devices we use. Your body is like a battery. Best of all, the energy in your body is renewable. Who needs a car to get around when you can walk, skateboard, or bike? Ignore the clothes dryer and hang clothes outside on a nice day.

Lightbulbs turn electricity they "eat" into some light. But some of the energy is wasted as heat. Fireflies turn the food they eat into total light. They do not heat up. They are the most efficient "lightbulbs" on Earth!

a Battery

Forget the leaf blower. Rake fall leaves into piles you can jump in!

Make Your

Stereos, tablets, and video games are fun, but they drain electricity. Make music with your hands, mouth, or feet.

These kids are having tons of fun without using electricity!

Own Fun

Read a book instead of watching TV. Play board games, tag, or sports. Saving electricity can be a lot of fun!

You can start your own pots-and-pans band!

Some game stations use more electricity than a refrigerator. A modern fridge uses as little as 350 kilowatts of electricity every year. Playing a video game on a plasma TV chews up 1,685 kilowatts a year!

Spark Energy-Smart Conversations

You have learned a lot about saving electricity. You also know that wasting power makes climate change worse. Now share what you know with others. You can inspire them to save energy, too!

Keep in mind, you are an amazing source of clean energy, too! The energy you use to pedal a bike for one hour is enough to power seven lightbulbs for the same amount of time.

Tell your friends
how they can save
electricity, too.

Project TGIF: Heat for

Are you wondering if kids really can make a difference? Cassandra Lin (near left) was in fifth grade when she discovered that some of her neighbors couldn't afford electricity to heat their homes in winter. Cassandra asked five of her friends to

collect used cooking oil from restaurants. They took the oil to a refinery, where it was changed into biodiesel. The power company turned the biodiesel, which is a clean-energy fuel, into free electricity for the families who needed it. Project Turn Grease Into Fuel (TGIF) was born!

Zap Electricity Vampires!

**Game station
289 kWh
lost per year**

**Laptop
144 kWh
lost per year**

**Plasma TV
1,452 kWh
lost per year**

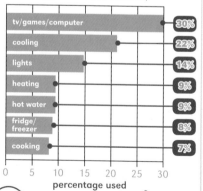

Primary Categories of Energy Use
(typical American household)

Category	Percentage
tv/games/computer	30%
cooling	22%
lights	14%
heating	9%
hot water	9%
fridge/freezer	8%
cooking	7%

0   5   10   15   20   25   30
percentage used

Note: Percentages do not add up
to 100 because of rounding.

Glossary

batteries (BAT-uh-reez): containers filled with chemicals that produce electrical power

incandescent (in-kan-DESS-uhnt): glowing with intense light and heat

pollute (puh-LOOT): contaminate or make dirty or impure

recycle (ree-SYE-kuhl): process old items so they can be used to make new products

Index

About the Author

Jenny Mason lives in Colorado, not far from where electricity was first made from a waterfall. Jenny loves to be out in the sun camping, playing tennis, hiking, or biking.

Facts for Now

Visit this Scholastic Web site for
more information on how to save electricity:

www.factsfornow.scholastic.com

Enter the keywords **Save Electricity**

Library of Congress Cataloging-in-Publication Data
Names: Mason, Jenny (Children's author)
Title: 10 things you can do to save electricity / by Jenny Mason.
Other titles: Ten things you can do to save electricity
Description: New York, NY : Children's Press, an imprint of Scholastic Inc.,
[2017] | Series: Rookie star. Make a difference | Includes bibliographical references and index.
Identifiers: LCCN 2016003771| ISBN 9780531226537 (library binding : alk. paper) | ISBN 9780531227596 (pbk. : alk. paper)
Subjects: LCSH: Electric power—Conservation—Juvenile literature. | Energy conservation—Juvenile literature.
Classification: LCC TJ163.35 .M37 2017 | DDC 333.791/6—dc23 LC record available at http://lccn.loc.gov/2016003771

Produced by Spooky Cheetah Press
Design by Judith Christ-Lafond

© 2017 by Scholastic Inc.

Printed in China 62

SCHOLASTIC, CHILDREN'S PRESS, ROOKIE STAR™, and associated logos are trademarks and/or registered trademarks of Scholastic Inc.

6 7 8 9 10 R 25 24 23 22 21 20 19 18

Photos ©: cover dress: nuiiko/Fotolia; cover girl: manley099/Getty Images; cover sky: Elenamiv/Shutterstock, Inc.; cover grass: Anan Kaewkhammul/Shutterstock, Inc.; cover yellow butterflies: kurga/Thinkstock; cover red butterflies: Cezar Serbanescu/Getty Images; cover lightbulb: bergamont/Shutterstock, Inc.; 2 top lights: Michael Kraus/Shutterstock, Inc.; 2-3 grass and throughout: djgis/Shutterstock, Inc.; 3 bottom right: NoraDoa/Fotolia; 3 top lights: Michael Kraus/Shutterstock, Inc.; 4, 5 background: chungking/Shutterstock, Inc.; 5 top: antoniotruzzi/Thinkstock; 5 center: GooGag/Shutterstock, Inc.; 5 bottom: Sarunyu_foto/Shutterstock, Inc.; 6 left: Marc Monés; 6 right: bopav/Thinkstock; 7 top: Tuned_In/ Thinkstock; 7 bottom: bopav/Thinkstock; 8: Artranq/Dreamstime; 9: ericsphotography/iStockphoto; 10, 11 background: freezingpicture/ Shutterstock, Inc.; 11 inset: Patrice Lange/Thinkstock; 12: Matej Kotula/Shutterstock, Inc.; 13: Ghislain & Marie David de Lossy/Getty Images; 14 bottom left: Serhiy Kobyakov/Fotolia; 14 computer: spaxiax/Fotolia; 14 screen: component/Shutterstock, Inc.; 15: Family Business/Fotolia; 16, 17 background: LiuNian/Thinkstock; 17 inset: Meinzahn/Thinkstock; 18: Benjamin A. Peterson/Mother Image/Fuse/Thinkstock; 19 bottom left: Lynne Sutherland/Alamy Images; 19 bottom right: Alexandra Grablewski/MCT/Newscom; 19 top crane: markobe/Fotolia; 19 top recycling: Skarie20/Dreamstime; 20: Phil Degginger/Alamy Images; 21: Ron Chapple/Media Bakery; 22: Pressmaster/Shutterstock, Inc.; 23 bottom: PeopleImages/Media Bakery; 23 top: GooGag/Shutterstock, Inc.; 24: jonas unruh/iStockphoto; 25: SerrNovik/Thinkstock; 26-27: Jason Lin; 28-29: Marc Monés; 30 top: rakim-/Thinkstock; 30 center top: Sarunyu_foto/Shutterstock, Inc.; 30 center bottom: Overcrew55/Shutterstock, Inc.; 30 bottom: Skarie20/Dreamstime.

Scholastic Inc., 557 Broadway, New York, NY 10012.